2/10

Nancy Winslow Parker

ORGANS!
HOW THEY WORK, FALL APART, AND CAN BE REPLACED (GASP!)

Greenwillow Books
An Imprint of HarperCollinsPublishers

To the doctors and nurses at New York-Presbyterian Hospital—N.W.P.

Author's Note

Several years ago I wasn't feeling well and had to go to the hospital. When I was examined, the doctor told me I had a diseased pancreas and that it would have to be removed.

"What is a pancreas?" I asked. The doctor told me it was an organ behind the belly button that produced insulin. Once it was removed, I would become an instant diabetic. I would be insulin-dependent, which means no cakes, pies, or ice cream—ever.

Since my recovery I have wondered why, at the age of sixty-seven, I knew nothing about the pancreas, not to mention the entire body—tubes, veins, pumps, organs, bones, filters, and on and on.

I have chosen to present in this book the anatomy of several vital organs in their simplest designs, with easy-to-understand descriptions and bright bubble gum colors. When you go visit Grandma in the hospital after her gallbladder operation, you will be prepared to assess the situation with no trouble at all, and Grandma will be so pleased and impressed.

I would like to thank Drs. Peter and Kathleen Hunt of Chattanooga, Tennessee, for their help and expertise in guiding this book. And thanks to Ellen A. Harrison, MD.

Organs!
How They Work, Fall Apart, and Can Be Replaced (Gasp!)
Copyright © 2009 by Nancy Winslow Parker
All rights reserved. Manufactured in China.
For information address HarperCollins Children's Books,
a division of HarperCollins Publishers, 10 East 53rd Street, New York, NY 10022.
www.harpercollinschildrens.com

Black pen, colored pencil, and watercolors were used to prepare the full-color art.
The text type is Cheltenham.

Library of Congress Cataloging-in-Publication Data

Parker, Nancy Winslow.
Organs! : how they work, fall apart, and can be replaced (gasp!) / by Nancy Winslow Parker.
p. cm.
"Greenwillow Books."
Includes index.
ISBN 978-0-688-15105-8 (trade bdg.) — ISBN 978-0-688-15106-5 (lib. bdg.)
1. Organs (Anatomy)—Juvenile literature. I. Title.
QM27.P265 2009   612'.028dc—22   2008020718

09 10 11 12 13 SCP First Edition 10 9 8 7 6 5 4 3 2 1

 Greenwillow Books

Contents

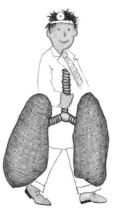

This is not a vital organ.

This is a pipe organ. It is a very old musical instrument and you can think of it as a musical respiratory system. The big pipe organ sucks in air through one or more of its valves and then pumps it out through the pipes, making sounds. People like to sing along to the music of an organ.

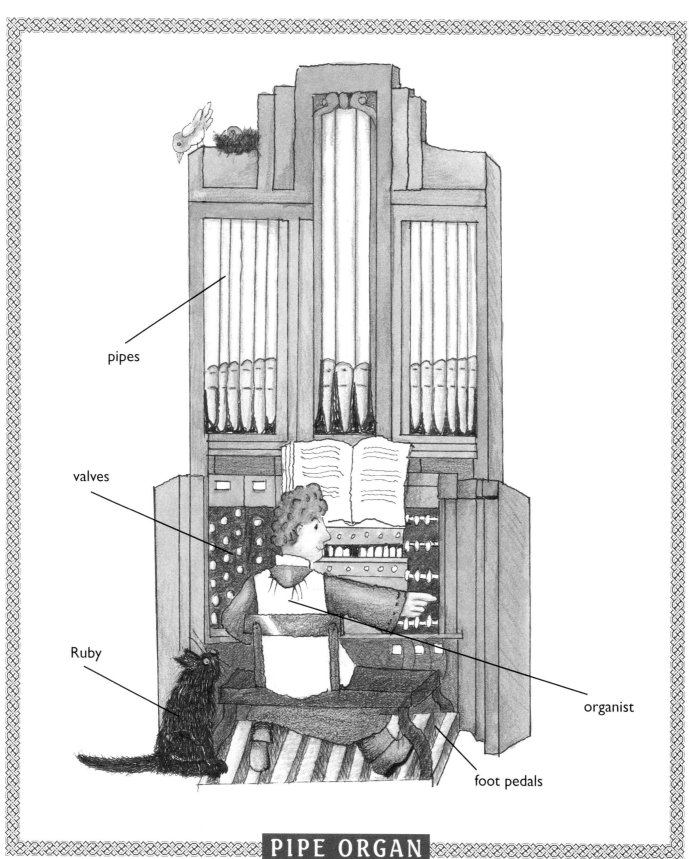

pipes

valves

Ruby

organist

foot pedals

PIPE ORGAN

This is a vital organ.

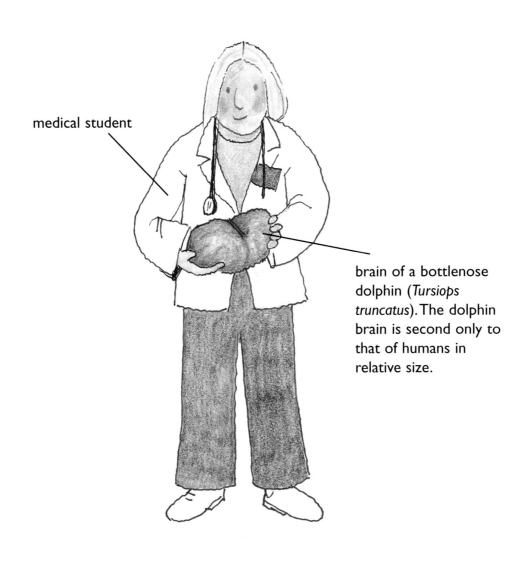

medical student

brain of a bottlenose dolphin (*Tursiops truncatus*). The dolphin brain is second only to that of humans in relative size.

WhAT iS A ViTAL ORGAN?

While some people might say music is vital to life, you could live without it. But unlike the pipe organ, vital organs are body parts that keep you breathing, digesting, thinking, and so much more.

People have been studying the human body for centuries. The ancient Greeks and Romans were the first to study the body big-time and named all the organs in their languages. They wanted to know how our insides work, how the body breaks down, and how to fix it. Over the years a method of study has evolved that makes the body easier to understand. It is the study of the body by systems. There are many systems, and we will explore seven major ones from head to toe.

All organ systems function both independently and cooperatively. Organs do not appear willy-nilly in the human body. They are in specific places. Everyone's brain is in the top of his or her head, for example, and the pancreas is just behind the stomach. The brain belongs to the nervous system and the pancreas to the digestive system, but they work together to keep your body running smoothly.

I think of the body as a Christmas tree, with veins like strings of beads and ropes and lights, organs scattered throughout like ornaments on branches, and a brain on top like a shining star.

Turn the page to read all about the fascinating organs of your body and how they work together to operate the most important thing in the world: you!

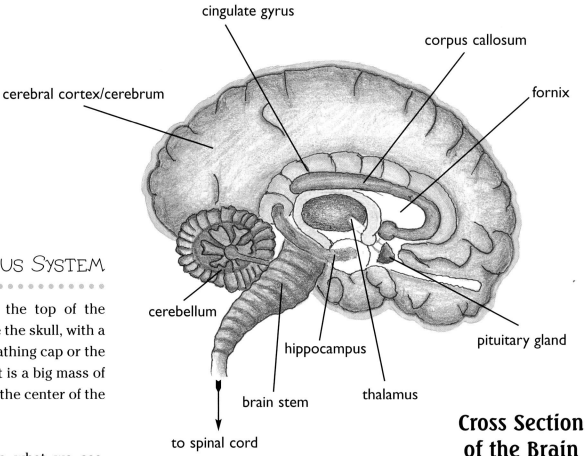

cingulate gyrus

corpus callosum

cerebral cortex/cerebrum

fornix

cerebellum

hippocampus

pituitary gland

brain stem

thalamus

to spinal cord

**Cross Section
of the Brain**

THE NERVOUS SYSTEM

The brain sits at the top of the human body, inside the skull, with a cover like a latex bathing cap or the rind of an orange. It is a big mass of nerve tissue and is the center of the nervous system.

The brain takes in what we see, hear, feel, and think. This is processed in specific sections of the brain, including the brain stem, and then the spinal cord shoots out instructions to the necessary organ systems, which will complete a task, such as picking up a ball and throwing it to a dog. The brain works very hard to direct our lives.

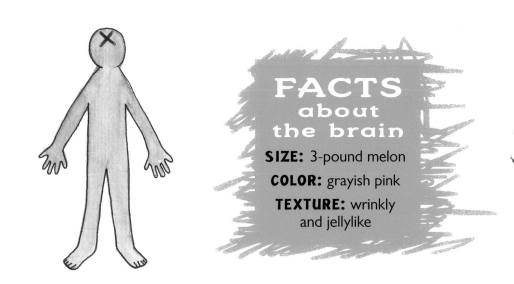

FACTS
about
the brain

SIZE: 3-pound melon

COLOR: grayish pink

TEXTURE: wrinkly
and jellylike

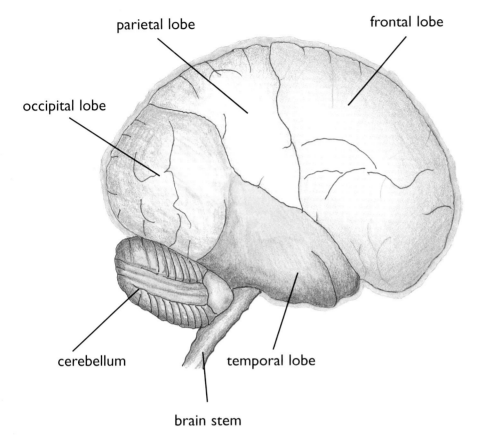

parietal lobe

frontal lobe

occipital lobe

cerebellum

temporal lobe

brain stem

THE LOBES OF THE BRAIN

The cerebrum is 85 percent of the brain's weight and is responsible for sending and receiving signals to make your body work. The top of the cerebrum—the cerebral cortex—is divided into four lobes that control different functions and often work together. Some of the frontal lobe's responsibilities include memory, decision making, and movement. The temporal lobe also helps control memory as well as speech and hearing. The parietal lobe determines our navigation and vision, while the occipital lobe helps process what we see. The cerebellum is what allows you to stand up straight, jump to make a basket, and balance on your bike. The brain stem takes care of all the important things your body needs to do, so you don't have to think about them: breathing, making sure your heart is beating, and circulating your blood.

TRUE STORY

In 1848 railroad worker Phineas Gage miraculously survived after a pipe accidentally went up through his cheekbone. His frontal lobe was damaged, so while he could still physically function, his personality had radically changed. He was now mean and unreliable, a big change from his old hardworking, responsible self.

PROTECTING THE BRAIN

Charlie offers to give his baby sister's teddy bear a ride on his handlebars. Of course, both he and Teddy wear bicycle helmets. Charlie knows that he has to protect his head and brain in case he falls off the bicycle. Without a helmet he could crack his skull and even harm his brain. Because the brain is soft and squishy, it needs the skull to protect it every day. A helmet is an extra layer of protection, looking out for both the skull and the brain within it. Everyone, even adults, needs to wear a helmet for activities like bike riding and sports. That's why you'll always see professional athletes like baseball players, football players, and skateboarders wearing helmets.

FACTS about brain weights

BABY: 1 pound
TODDLER: 2.5 pounds
SIX-YEAR-OLD: 3 pounds
ADULT: 3 pounds
TEDDY BEAR: 0 pounds

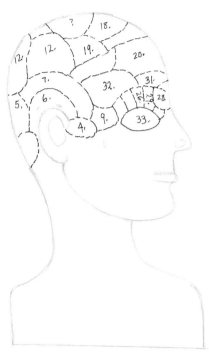

Phrenologists used white porcelain models of heads, like the one illustrated here, to analyze the bumps and what they meant. On the models, the head was divided into many labeled sections, and each one represented a different idea, like hope, time, and language.

PHRENOLOGY

Phrenology is a theory about studying the brain that became popular in the early nineteenth century. It was considered science then, but we know now it was first-class quackery. People understood that human behavior was directed by the brain, but some actually believed that the doctor/scientist could tell a person's character by feeling the bumps on his or her head! They thought the bumps were formed from use, disuse, and overuse of different sections of the brain. For example, in the brain of a person who hated music, that music-centered section of the brain would shrink, causing a valley in the top of the head. But if that person overused the science section of his or her brain, it got big, creating a hill. Today we know that reading the peaks and valleys of a skull with one's fingers results in nothing more than a relaxing scalp massage.

ALZHEIMER'S DISEASE

One of the pioneers in the study of the brain was Alois Alzheimer (1864–1915), a German neurologist. He discovered that premature senility could lead to a grave disorder of the brain, in which mental powers failed. An Alzheimer's patient can have poor judgment, difficulty speaking, a change of personality, and memory loss. About one in seven Americans over age seventy-one will get Alzheimer's in his or her lifetime. Luckily, scientists are working hard every day to find out more. The more we understand about how different parts of the brain work, the closer we will get to cures for diseases such as Alzheimer's.

THE RESPIRATORY SYSTEM

The respiratory system is the breathing machine in your body. It consists of the nose, the throat, and the lungs. The air we breathe enters the body via the nose and mouth, travels down the windpipe (trachea), and enters the lungs. In the lungs oxygen in the air is exchanged with carbon dioxide, which we don't need, and the carbon dioxide leaves the body the way the air came in, via the nose and mouth.

A doctor who specializes in the lungs is a called a pulmonologist. An otolaryngologist, or ENT—an ear, nose, and throat doctor—specializes in those parts.

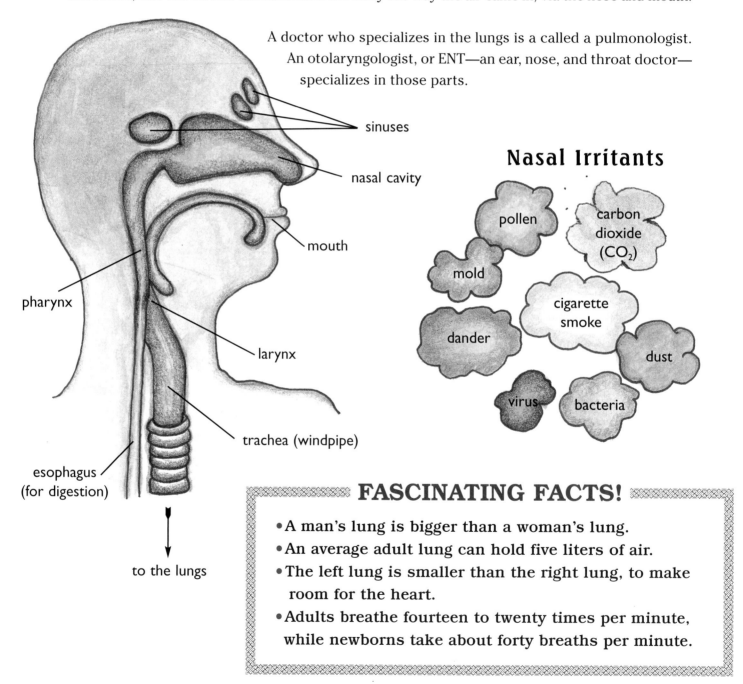

- sinuses
- nasal cavity
- mouth
- pharynx
- larynx
- trachea (windpipe)
- esophagus (for digestion)
- to the lungs

Nasal Irritants

- pollen
- carbon dioxide (CO_2)
- mold
- cigarette smoke
- dander
- dust
- virus
- bacteria

FASCINATING FACTS!

- A man's lung is bigger than a woman's lung.
- An average adult lung can hold five liters of air.
- The left lung is smaller than the right lung, to make room for the heart.
- Adults breathe fourteen to twenty times per minute, while newborns take about forty breaths per minute.

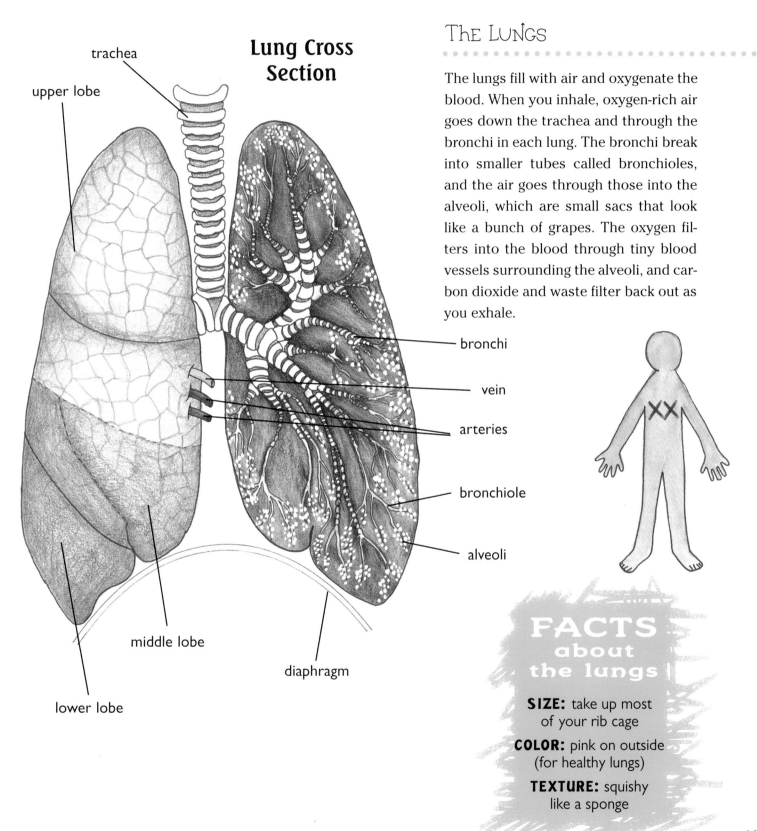

Lung Cross Section

trachea

upper lobe

bronchi

vein

arteries

bronchiole

alveoli

middle lobe

diaphragm

lower lobe

THE LUNGS

The lungs fill with air and oxygenate the blood. When you inhale, oxygen-rich air goes down the trachea and through the bronchi in each lung. The bronchi break into smaller tubes called bronchioles, and the air goes through those into the alveoli, which are small sacs that look like a bunch of grapes. The oxygen filters into the blood through tiny blood vessels surrounding the alveoli, and carbon dioxide and waste filter back out as you exhale.

FACTS about the lungs

SIZE: take up most of your rib cage

COLOR: pink on outside (for healthy lungs)

TEXTURE: squishy like a sponge

13

THE NASAL SINUSES

Aunt Muriel loves her job working as a baker, but unfortunately she has very sensitive sinuses. Her allergy to baking flour leads to sneezing, watery eyes, and a sore throat for poor Muriel. Luckily, she has a great ENT doctor, who can help her with her sinus problems related to work, as well as any head colds, coughs, or runny noses she may get throughout the year.

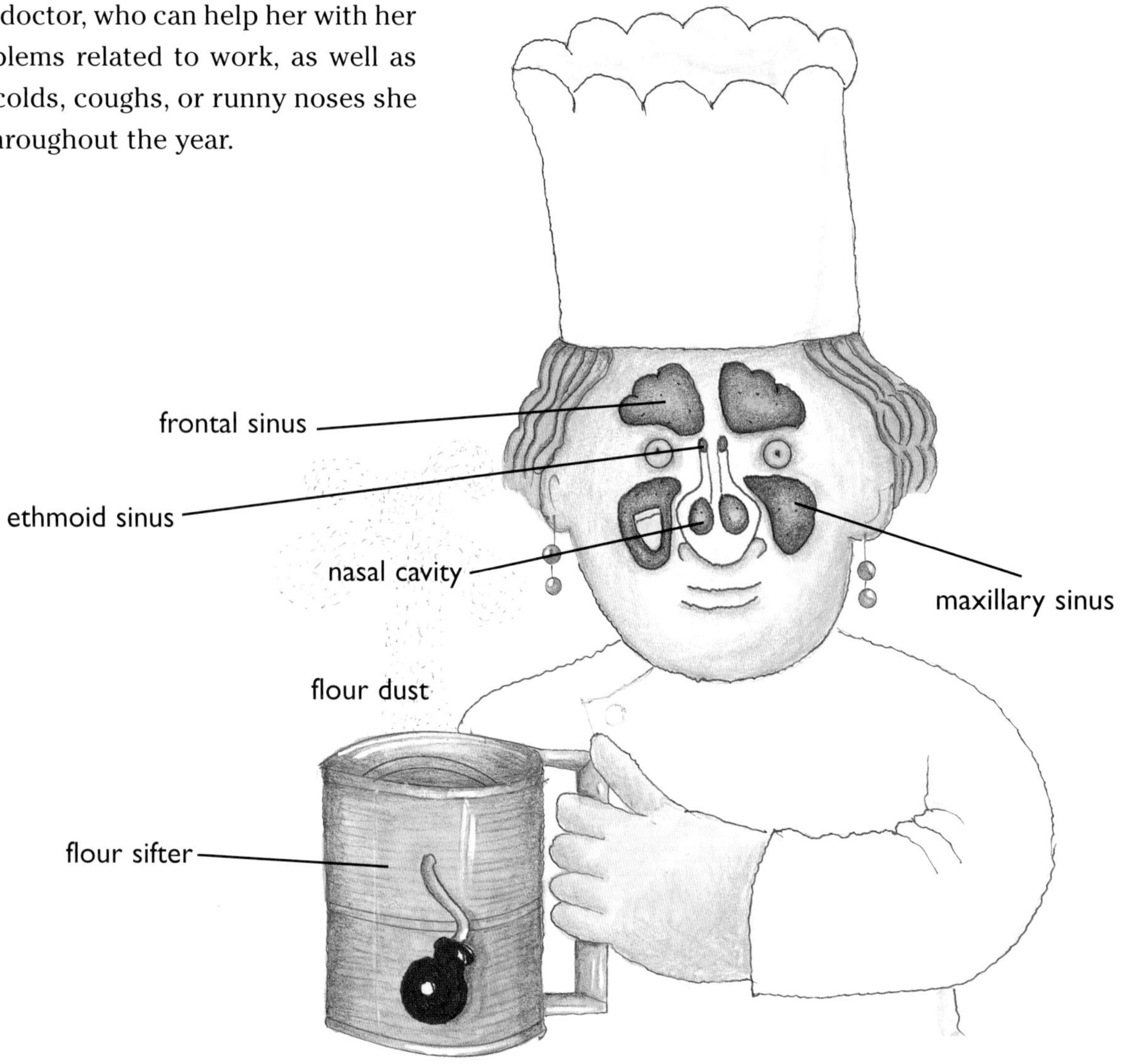

frontal sinus

ethmoid sinus

nasal cavity

maxillary sinus

flour dust

flour sifter

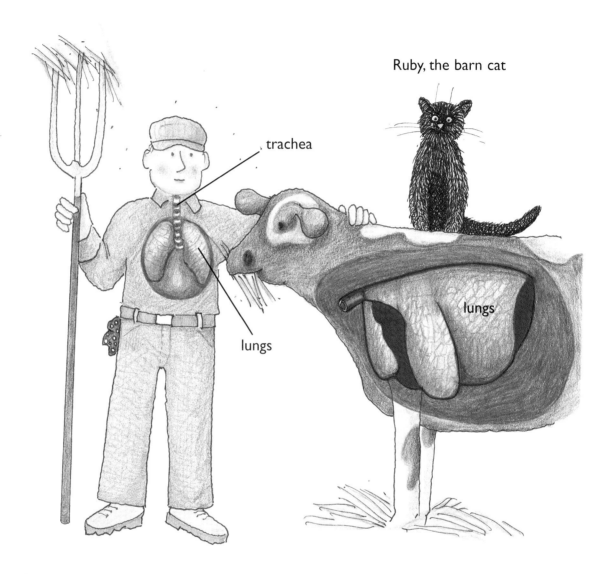

Ruby, the barn cat

trachea

lungs

lungs

LUNGS ON THE FARM

As you might expect, a cow's lungs are much bigger than human lungs, because of their difference in body size. However, their lungs also have similarities. Both species are considered relatively inactive compared with other animals, such as dogs and horses, and their lungs' diffusing capacity—a measure of the lung's ability to process the gases it inhales—is lower than that of those other animals because of their lower activity rate. Another way in which they are similar is their susceptibility to lung diseases that are caused by their environment. Despite the name, both farmers and cows can get farmer's lung, an inflammation of the lung tissue that is caused by moldy hay or other farm products. For farmers who worry about this problem, there are precautions they can take, including wearing a mask or taking prescribed medicines.

The Circulatory System

The circulatory system comprises the veins, arteries, heart, and spleen. This system's job is to keep blood flowing. Blood supplies oxygen and nutrients to every part of our bodies through veins and arteries. Arteries carry blood away from the heart, and veins carry it toward the heart. The circulatory system is also important when we are sick or injured. It sends disease-fighting agents to fight off viruses and bacteria, and it sends cells that clot the blood to keep wounds from bleeding too much.

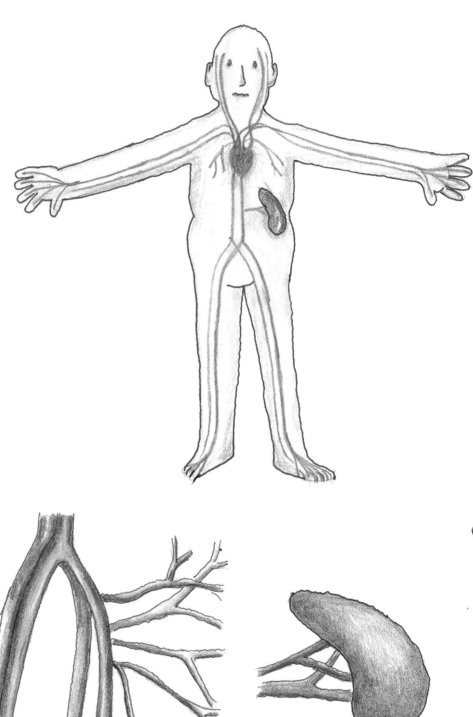

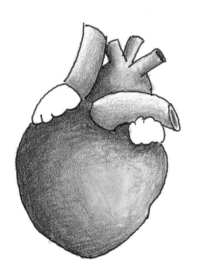

Heart

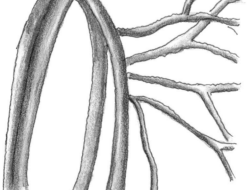

Arteries and Veins

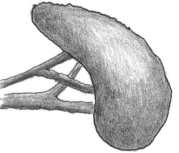

Spleen

16

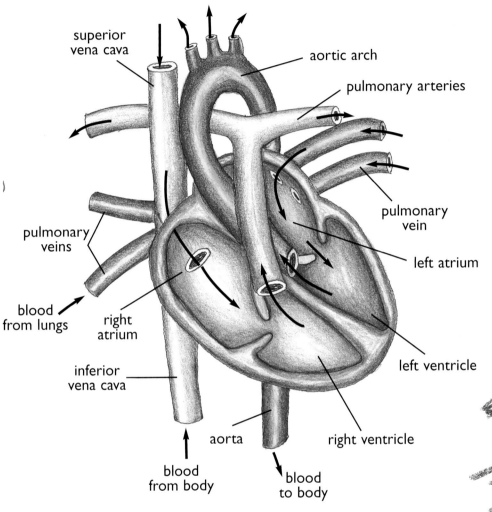

superior
vena cava

aortic arch

pulmonary arteries

pulmonary
vein

left atrium

pulmonary
veins

blood
from lungs

right
atrium

inferior
vena cava

left ventricle

aorta

right ventricle

blood
from body

blood
to body

HOW THE HEART WORKS

The heart is responsible for receiving blood from the veins, sending it to the lungs for oxygen, and pumping it out to the body through the arteries. The heart has four sections. The upper two sections of the heart are called the atria. The lower two are called the ventricles. Blood comes into the heart through the atria and leaves through the ventricles.

FACTS about the heart

SIZE: a fist (1 pound)
COLOR: dark red
TEXTURE: slimy

BLOOD FLOW IN THE BODY

body ⟶ right atrium ⟶ right ventricle ⟶

pulmonary arteries ⟶ lungs ⟶ pulmonary veins

⟶ left atrium ⟶ left ventricle ⟶ body

Canine hearts are similar to human hearts in many ways, but they are larger relative to their bodies, as are their lungs. This is why dogs can be so energetic; their oversize hearts and lungs give them lots of energy. But while humans must be more careful about heart attacks, dogs and other animals are prime targets for heartworms. Heartworms are between six and fourteen inches long. A dog's heart provides the ideal living conditions for a heartworm to breed.

When Elvis, a bluetick coonhound, was four years old, he came down with heartworm disease. Elvis's owner suspected Elvis had heartworms and took him to the veterinarian, who kept Elvis in the clinic until the worms were killed and eliminated from his body.

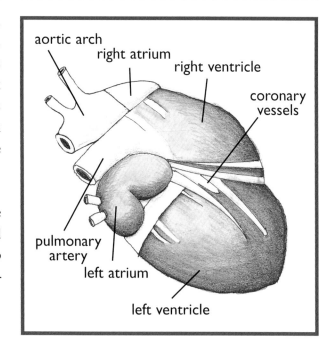

Dog (*Canis lupus familiaris*)

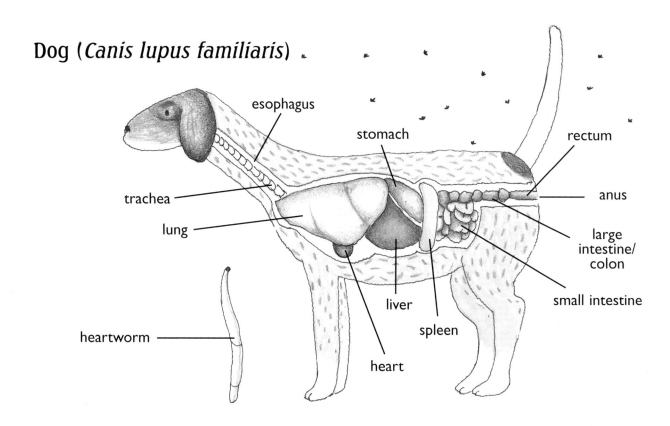

Diseased Artery

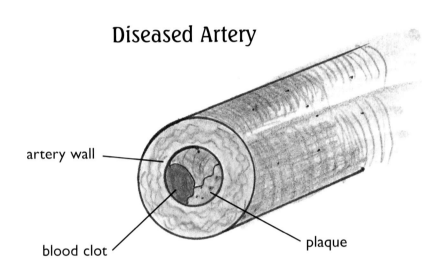

artery wall

blood clot

plaque

HEART ATTACKS

HEART ATTACK RISK FACTORS

heredity
smoking
inactivity
obesity
diabetes
high blood pressure
high cholesterol
age

One day Dad experienced severe pains in his chest. He rushed to the hospital, where doctors determined he was having a heart attack. A heart attack is caused by a clogged artery, which affects the blood supply to the heart. This is a very serious condition that can cause permanent damage, and it's very important to receive treatment fast. The artery blockages are fatty deposits, called plaque, that build up inside the artery. While the likelihood of developing plaque can be hereditary, there are other risk factors that are easy to avoid. Decreasing your risk factors can help prevent a heart attack. In Dad's case, the doctors have several surgical options to help his heart, and once he's out of the hospital he'll have to be very careful about diet and exercise, and he'll have to take medicines his doctor prescribes for him.

THE SPLEEN

The spleen may be the most ignored and misunderstood of all the organs. It is located behind and to the left of the stomach, under the diaphragm. The spleen has three important functions: It filters blood from the heart, it fights infections from viruses and bacteria, and the antibodies in its white blood cells kill viruses and infections.

FACTS about the spleen

SIZE: 5 inches long (like a fist)

COLOR: hyacinth blue/dark purple

TEXTURE: slippery coat, pulpy inside, spongy to touch

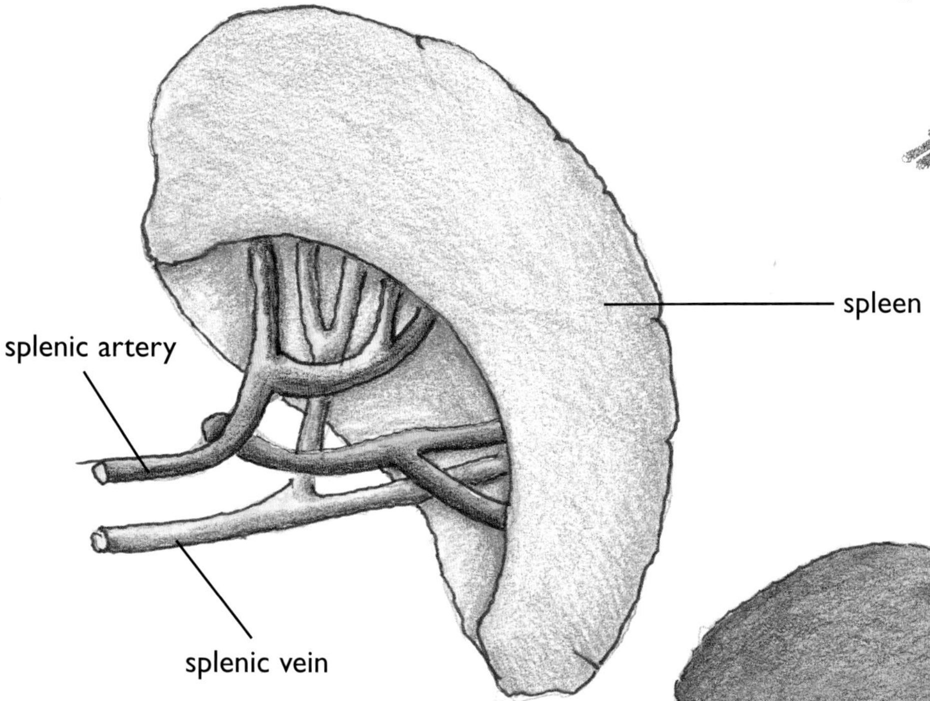

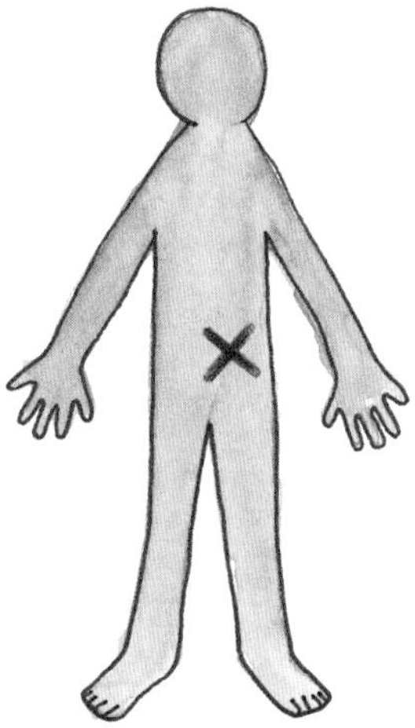

splenic artery

splenic vein

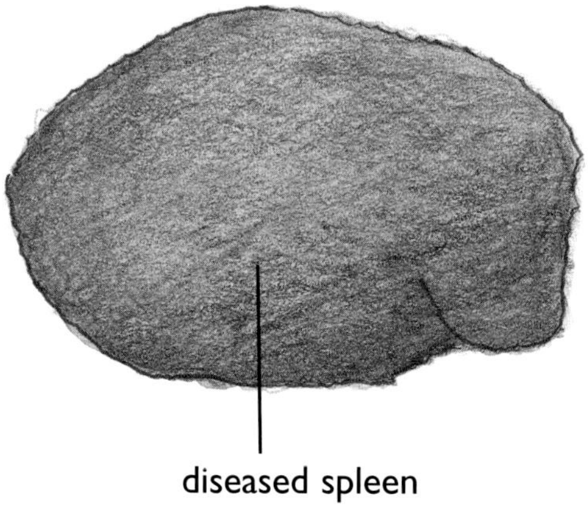

spleen

diseased spleen

PLAY IT SAFE

During a football game, Cousin Will received a hard blow that ruptured his spleen. It became a beehive of activity fighting to survive. He was rushed to the hospital, where tests revealed that there was a buildup of blood and the organ was deteriorating. The doctors decided to remove the spleen in an operation called a splenectomy.

Though the spleen does important work, it can be removed if it is damaged, and other organs will take over its jobs. A spleen may be removed if it suffers trauma, becomes overactive and filters out the good stuff along with the bad, or develops cancer. A doctor will help patients adjust by providing them with medicines to take the place of the spleen's illness-fighting role.

21

THE DIGESTIVE SYSTEM

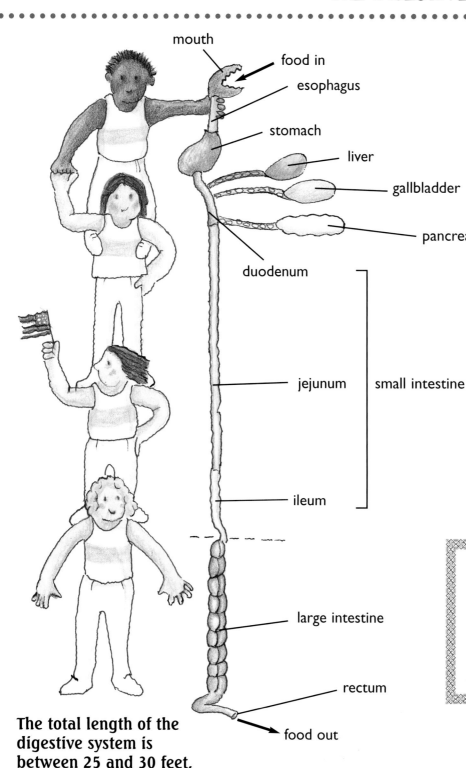

mouth

food in

esophagus

stomach

liver

gallbladder

pancreas

duodenum

jejunum — small intestine

ileum

large intestine

rectum

food out

The total length of the digestive system is between 25 and 30 feet.

FASCINATING FACTS!

It takes the digestive system six hours to digest a normal meal of a grilled cheese sandwich, apple, and cranberry juice.

The Digestive Path

The digestive system begins with your mouth. Here your food of choice—ice cream or nuts, barbecued steak or boiled chicken—is chewed and swallowed. When you swallow, the food moves down the pharynx and through the esophagus into the stomach.

At the junction of the esophagus and the stomach is a sphincter muscle that closes up tight to keep the stomach acids from backing up into the esophagus. If this "trapdoor" stops opening and closing properly, stomach juices can escape and cause coughing, pain, and difficulty in eating and digesting. This is called Gastroesophageal Reflux Disease, or GERD.

HARMFUL IF SWALLOWED!

buttons
bones
unchewed meat
pennies

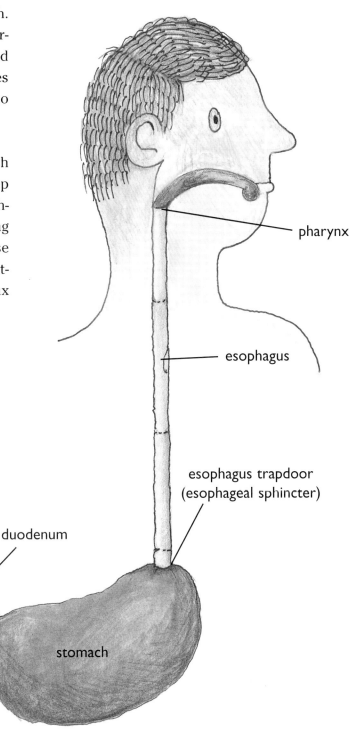

pharynx

esophagus

esophagus trapdoor
(esophageal sphincter)

duodenum

stomach

THE LIVER

The liver is the largest internal organ; a complex chemical factory, food storehouse, and refinery. This Mr. Big of the organ world helps digest food, filter poisons like alcohol, and make new cells. It produces bile, a green-brown fluid, which aids in digestion and is stored in the gallbladder.

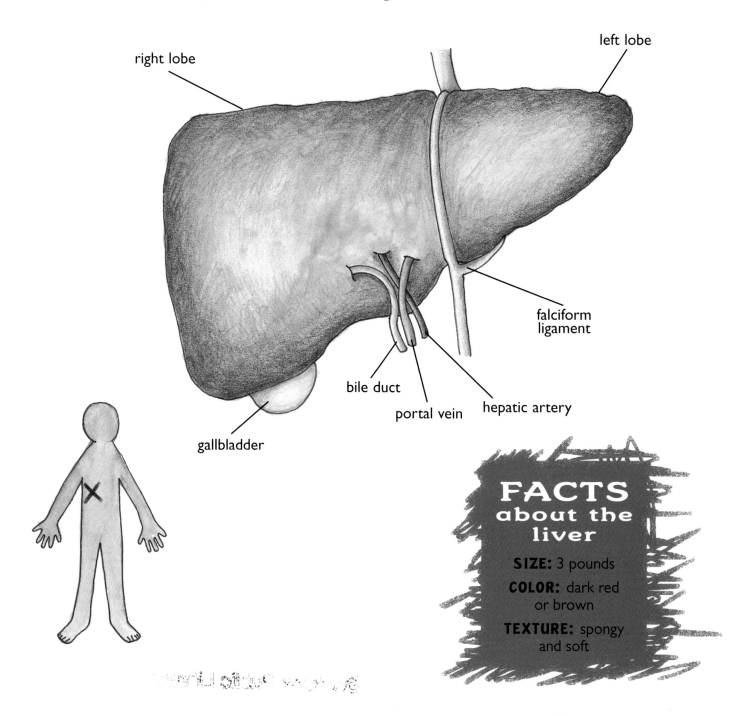

right lobe

left lobe

falciform ligament

bile duct

portal vein

hepatic artery

gallbladder

FACTS about the liver

SIZE: 3 pounds

COLOR: dark red or brown

TEXTURE: spongy and soft

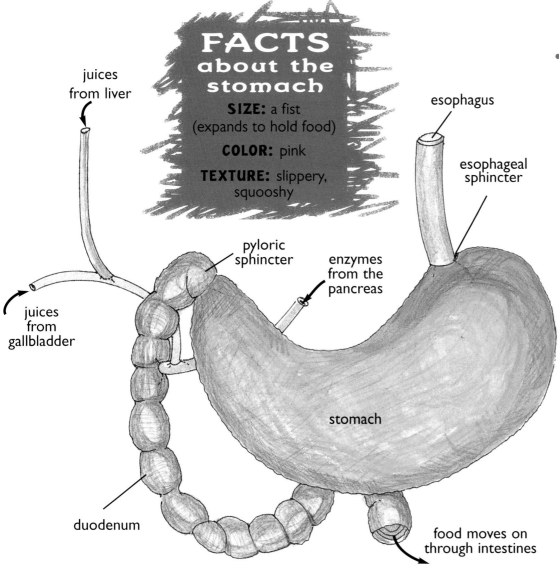

FACTS about the stomach

SIZE: a fist (expands to hold food)

COLOR: pink

TEXTURE: slippery, squooshy

juices from liver

juices from gallbladder

pyloric sphincter

enzymes from the pancreas

esophagus

esophageal sphincter

stomach

duodenum

food moves on through intestines

THE STOMACH

Food comes into the stomach from the esophagus. When the stomach is empty, its walls touch, but as food enters, it expands to hold the food. The stomach contains acids and digestive enzymes, which break down food into pieces that are small enough to go into the small intestine. Once broken down, the digested food goes through the pyloric sphincter and into the small intestine, where most of the nutrients are absorbed into the body. Juices from the liver, gallbladder, and pancreas help further digest the food as it moves through the duodenum, the first part of the small intestine.

TRUE STORY!

In the early 1800s a Canadian trapper was accidentally shot in the chest, leaving a huge hole in his body. Amazingly, the man lived and his organs healed. But the hole that led right into his stomach never fully closed up! This allowed his doctor to actually observe the digestive system at work and learn incredible new things.

You Can't Live Without a Liver!

There are countless different liver diseases, many of which are caused by contact with chemicals, environmental pollutants, and drugs and alcohol. The famous baseball player Mickey Mantle suffered from an alcohol-related disease called cirrhosis. Late in his life he realized how much he had damaged his liver, as well as the importance of treating one's body well. Unfortunately, even a liver transplant wasn't enough to undo the damage he had done to his body. Before he died, he founded the Mickey Mantle Foundation to raise awareness about organ donation and transplants.

Luckily, many liver diseases are preventable if you take proper care of yourself, and researchers are always looking for new cures. A liver doctor is called a hepatologist. One hepatologist who made a big impact on the study of livers was Dame Sheila Sherlock. She researched ways to diagnose and treat all kinds of liver disorders. She worked in a famous clinic in England that many doctors still visit today. Even more remarkable was that Dr. Sherlock studied medicine during a time when few women did so.

Mickey Mantle
7 New York
Yankees
1931–1995

Dame Sheila Sherlock
Liver expert
1918–2001

THE SMALL INTESTINE

Food enters the small intestine from the stomach and travels the entire length of the slippery, folded, twisted tube to the cecum for the rest of the digestive journey. The small intestine folds eight hundred times and is actually longer than the large intestine, but is called small because its diameter is smaller. The small intestine further breaks down digested food and also absorbs nutrients like vitamins, fats, and sugars.

FACTS about the small intestine

SIZE: 13–23 feet long

COLOR: grayish purple

TEXTURE: slimy

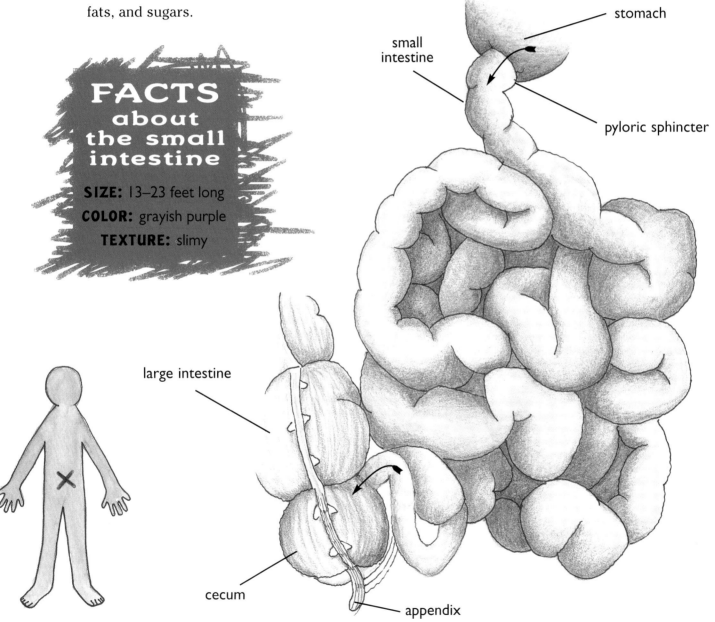

stomach

small intestine

pyloric sphincter

large intestine

cecum

appendix

THE LARGE INTESTINE

Another name for the large intestine is the colon. Some parts of food have no nutrients the body can use, and so they leave the small intestine undigested and move on to the large intestine. As this waste is moved along, any water in it is reabsorbed. Whatever is left moves to the bowel and exits through the rectum.

FACTS about the large intestine

SIZE: 5 feet long

COLOR: dark red

TEXTURE: slimy

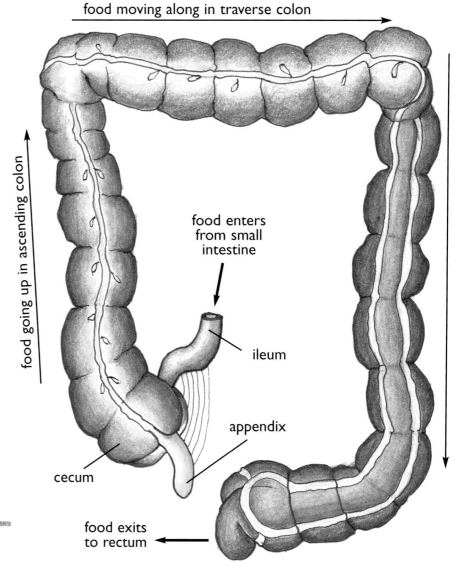

food moving along in traverse colon

food going up in ascending colon

food moving down in descending colon

food enters from small intestine

ileum

appendix

cecum

food exits to rectum

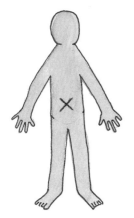

CROHN'S DISEASE

Crohn's disease causes inflammation of the intestinal wall. Symptoms can include fatigue, weight loss, joint pain, skin lesions, chronic diarrhea, fever, and abdominal cramps and can affect both children and grown-ups. This disease is named for **Dr. Burrill B. Crohn**, who discovered it. Doctors are able to treat the disease effectively with medicines and surgery, and researchers continue to look for a cure.

Is The Appendix A Vital Organ?

The appendix is found where the large and small intestines meet. Though every person has one, it doesn't seem to serve any purpose. In fact, if there are problems with it, it can be safely removed without causing any harm to the patient and his or her normal bodily functions. It is, however, important for appendicitis to be diagnosed quickly, because if left untreated, the appendix may burst, which can lead to blood poisoning.

burst
appendix

Honk!
Honk!

When Uncle Wilmer first felt a terrible pain in his right side, he thought it might be from stress. He is a policeman who directs traffic on a busy city street, enduring danger, noise, noxious fumes, and aggressive people and pets. Luckily, he went to the hospital right away, and the doctors discovered he was suffering from appendicitis. Uncle Wilmer's appendix had not burst, so it was safely removed, and in three days he was back at the corner of Forty-second Street and Eighth Avenue in New York City directing traffic.

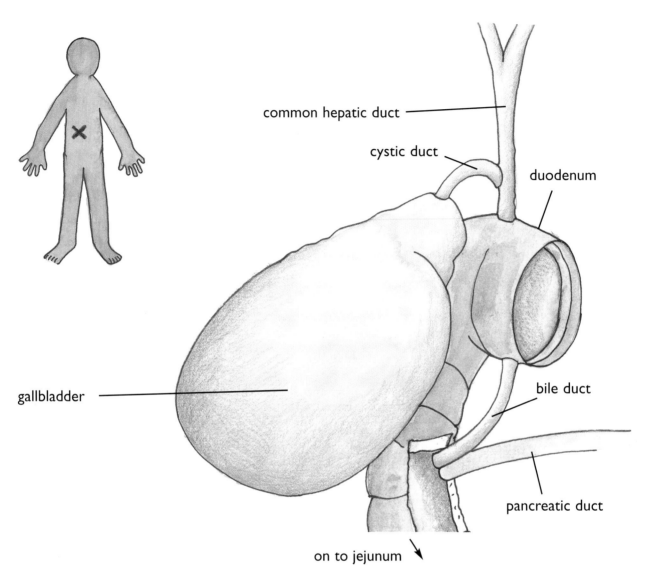

common hepatic duct

cystic duct

duodenum

gallbladder

bile duct

pancreatic duct

on to jejunum

THE GALLBLADDER

The gallbladder holds bile, a bitter-tasting fluid produced by the liver, until it is discharged into the small intestine. Once in the small intestine, bile helps in the digestion of fats.

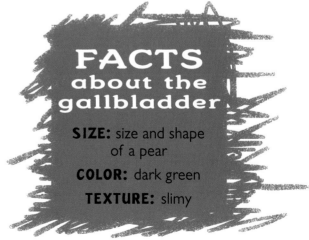

FACTS about the gallbladder

SIZE: size and shape of a pear

COLOR: dark green

TEXTURE: slimy

THE PANCREAS

· ·

The pancreas is a large, elongated gland. It is tucked under the stomach and backs into the duodenum. The pancreas produces insulin, an enzyme to aid digestion, which is squirted through the pancreatic duct to the duodenum. Alcohol, tobacco, gallstones, and obesity can weaken the pancreas.

In addition to the digestive system, the pancreas is part of the endocrine system, which comprises the small organs in our bodies that produce and release hormones. This system plays a very important role in metabolism, tissues, the body's constant growth and change, and often affects moods and emotions.

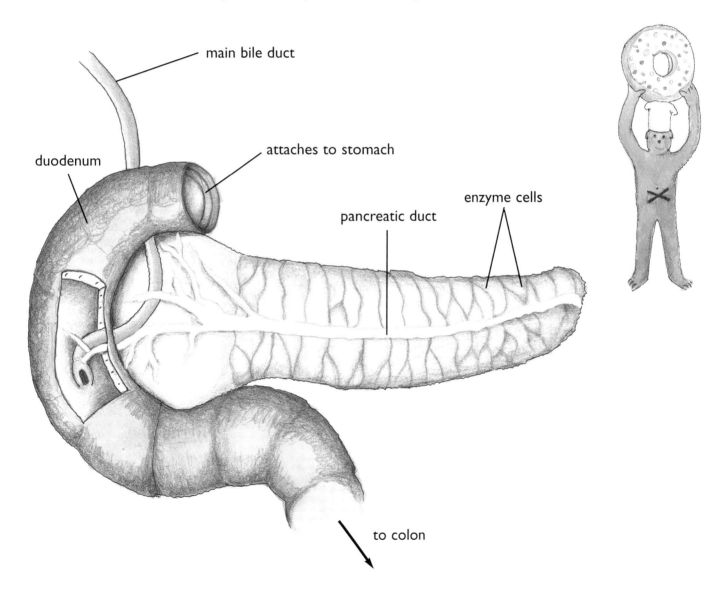

main bile duct

duodenum

attaches to stomach

enzyme cells

pancreatic duct

to colon

GALLSTONES

Two members of our family have problems with sweets. Mom has a formidable sweet tooth; she loves desserts and fatty foods. This may be part of the reason she developed gallstones, which are hardened clumps of bile that can range in size from a pencil point to a Ping-Pong ball. Some gallstones can pass through the body, but unfortunately, Mom's were bad enough that she had to have her gallbladder removed. Most people can function fine without gallbladders, but Mom will have to be careful and eat a diet high in fiber and low in fat, drink lots of water, and avoid caffeine.

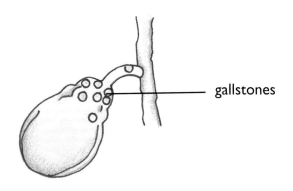

gallstones

DIABETES

Aunt Muriel has to monitor her diet for a very different reason: she has diabetes. For people with diabetes, the pancreas does not produce enough insulin to regulate the body's blood sugar level. Insulin must be taken manually to help balance the levels and reach a normal blood sugar level. A piece of chocolate cake can cause the blood sugar to shoot up to a very dangerous level for a diabetic. It's important for diabetics to monitor their blood sugar levels, through both diet and insulin use. Muriel has to be very careful, since she is surrounded by tempting sweets all day, but as long as she is responsible and aware, she can lead a normal life.

THE URINARY SYSTEM

Most people are born with two kidneys, one on each side of the spine, toward the back of the body. The kidney's main job is to act as a filter for the blood. Blood enters the kidneys through a renal artery. It is processed by bushlike tufts (glomerular capillaries), which keep the necessary liquid and remove excess fluid and waste. This excess is called urine, and it departs the kidneys through the ureter. Urine enters the bladder and waits until you tell it to go. The bladder excretes one and one-half quarts of urine per day.

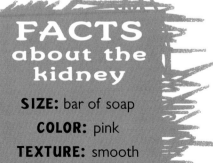

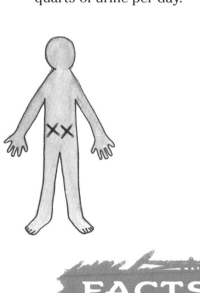

FACTS about the kidney

SIZE: bar of soap
COLOR: pink
TEXTURE: smooth

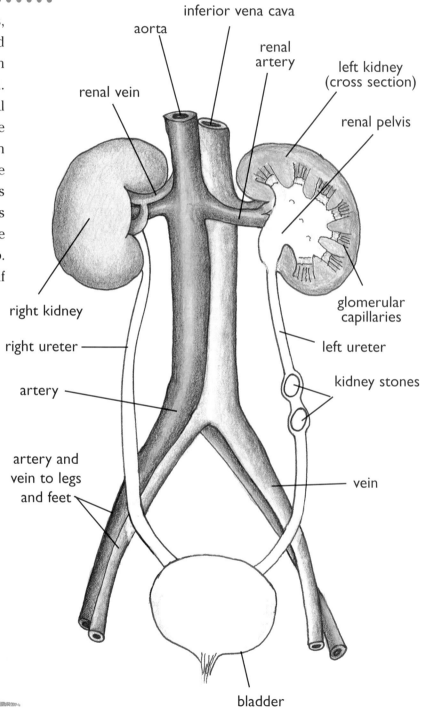

aorta

inferior vena cava

renal artery

left kidney (cross section)

renal vein

renal pelvis

right kidney

glomerular capillaries

right ureter

left ureter

artery

kidney stones

artery and vein to legs and feet

vein

bladder

HORSESHOE KIDNEYS

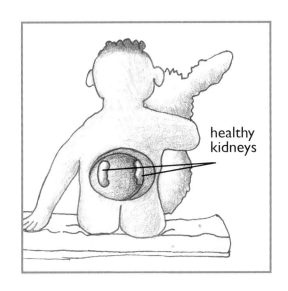

healthy kidneys

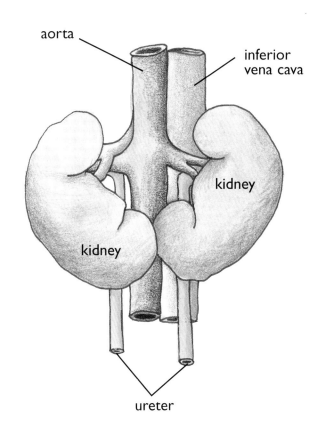

aorta

inferior vena cava

kidney

kidney

ureter

CAN YOU LIVE WITH ONLY ONE KIDNEY?

Though the body functions best with two kidneys, it is possible to live very well with just one. Sometimes people are born with just one kidney, and other times a person's kidneys are fused together into one. This is called a horseshoe kidney. Occasionally, as in the gallbladder, small stones of mineral buildup can form in the kidneys. They must pass through the ureter to the bladder and can be very painful. For any of these problems, people can see a nephrologist, a doctor who specializes in the kidneys.

THE BLADDER

The bladder is an elastic organ that holds and releases urine from the kidneys. The urine flows into the bladder through the ureters and exits out through the urethra. The muscle that you use to hold urine in until you are ready to go is called the urethral sphincter.

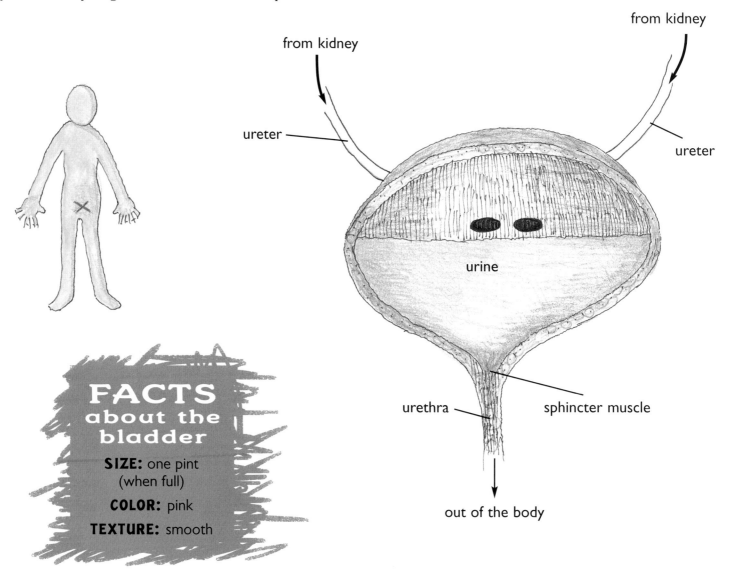

from kidney

from kidney

ureter

ureter

urine

FACTS about the bladder

SIZE: one pint (when full)

COLOR: pink

TEXTURE: smooth

urethra

sphincter muscle

out of the body

WhEN YoU GoTTA Go, YoU GoTTA Go!

The average bladder holds ten to twenty ounces of urine, roughly the amount of a can of soda! When the bladder is only half full, you will feel the urge to go. Learning how to know when to go is a normal part of growing up and is different for every kid. Grown-ups may also have problems with this, especially as they get older, because the brain signal and their muscular control get weaker. Grandma should not have waited so long after drinking three cups of coffee to go to the bathroom. She has had to run out of the second act of her favorite Broadway play, but with luck she won't miss too much. People with bladder problems can see a urologist, a doctor who specializes in the urinary system, to find out what treatments are available.

Playbill

THE SKELETAL SYSTEM

The adult skeletal system is made up of 206 bones of all different shapes and sizes. It holds up the body and keeps various organs, blood vessels, and other systems in place. It also helps us move.

Bones are made up of many cells called osteocytes, osteoblasts, and osteoclasts. The outside is hard, but the inside is made of a spongy red and yellow marrow. The yellow marrow stores fat and releases it to other parts of the body when needed. The red marrow is tissue that makes red and white blood cells and platelets.

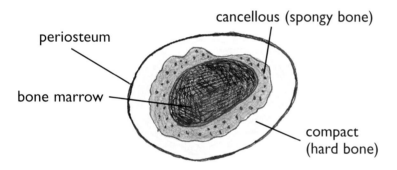

periosteum

cancellous (spongy bone)

bone marrow

compact (hard bone)

Cross Section of Bone

FASCINATING FACTS!

Sailors in the nineteenth century carved beautiful pictures on whale bones and teeth, as well as walrus tusks. Called scrimshaw, it was a highly prized art form. Many other cultures created art out of animal bones and ivory (teeth and tusks) as well; they include the Inuit of Alaska and the Maori of New Zealand. Elephant tusks were also carved in parts of Africa and Asia where elephants were in abundance. However, to protect endangered species from poachers, the sale of scrimshaw was made illegal worldwide.

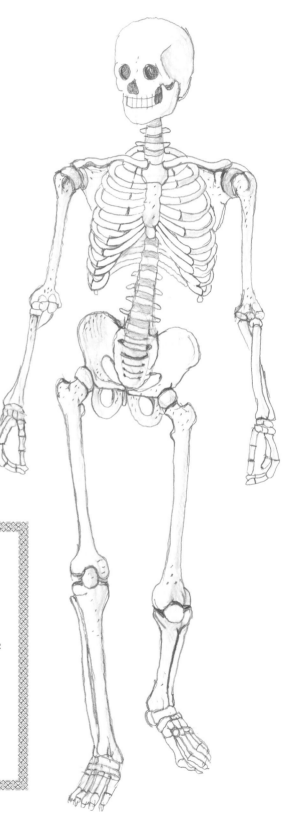

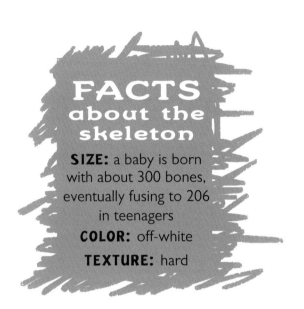

FACTS about the skeleton

SIZE: a baby is born with about 300 bones, eventually fusing to 206 in teenagers

COLOR: off-white

TEXTURE: hard

BREAKS AND FRACTURES

Though bones are very strong, they can break if they suffer trauma, such as a fall from a tree, a crash off a skateboard, or an accident while playing sports. Kids' bones are more pliable than adult bones, so they often don't break entirely through; this is called a greenstick fracture, and is quicker to heal. When Charlie was thrown off his skateboard, however, he wasn't wearing any protective gear, and his broken leg was bad enough that he needed surgery. Luckily, it was a simple fracture of the tibia, which the doctors easily repaired.

Greenstick fracture

Simple fracture of the tibia

THE INTEGUMENTARY SYSTEM

You might not think of the skin as an organ, but in fact it's the biggest one of all! It wraps around all the other organs and prevents them from falling out of the body. Skin works to keep our bodies healthy. It produces vitamin D, it keeps water in and out, and it protects against bacteria. The skin signals the brain about cold, heat, touch, pain, and pressure on its surface, so that we shiver, sweat, or otherwise react to different conditions.

The skin has three layers. The top layer is the epidermis. It serves as the first layer of protection from the sun and other elements and is constantly regenerating. The second layer is the dermis, which has some elasticity so that it can help absorb stress and strain for the body. It also houses hair follicles, sweat glands, and blood vessels. The third layer is the subcutaneous tissue, which contains fat and connective tissue. Too much fat in this layer is bad, but everyone needs some fat to keep him or her warm in the winter and to absorb shock if he or she falls down.

Lots of Stuff in Skin!

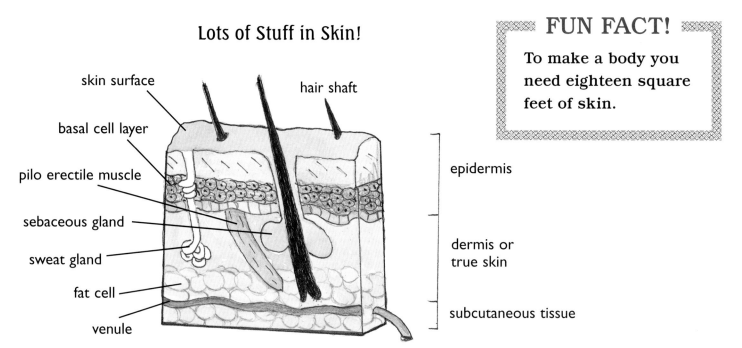

skin surface
basal cell layer
pilo erectile muscle
sebaceous gland
sweat gland
fat cell
venule
hair shaft
epidermis
dermis or true skin
subcutaneous tissue

FUN FACT!

To make a body you need eighteen square feet of skin.

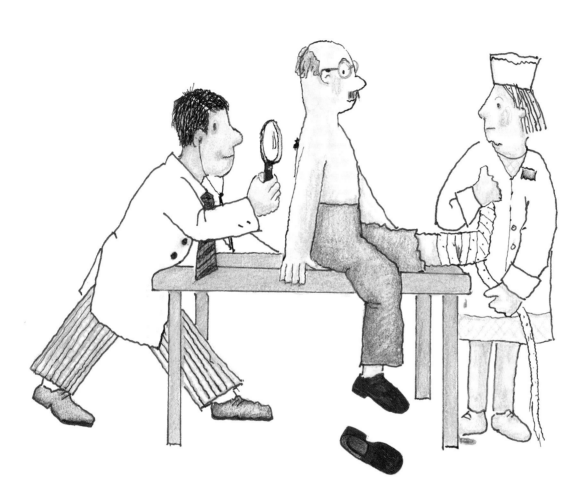

SPOT THOSE SPOTS!

Grandpa went to the emergency room after being bitten by a dog. He was worried about the deep wound and about getting rabies. The doctors bandaged up his leg, and luckily, the dog was tested and declared rabies free. But in their overall checkup of Grandpa, the doctors discovered a suspicious black spot on his back. Because Grandpa spent years and years in the sun without sunblock, he had developed a melanoma. This is a rare form of skin cancer, which presents itself as a strangely shaped discoloration of the skin. It's important to catch things like this early, so they can be removed before the cancer spreads. Maybe Grandpa should thank that dog for biting him!

PAST–ANCIENT EGYPT

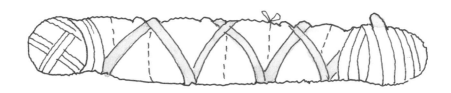

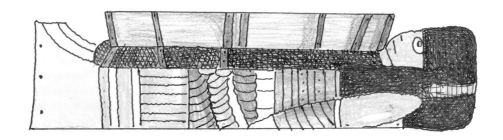

The ancient Egyptians are famous for how well they preserved dead bodies as mummies. The preparation of the body for the afterlife was a sacred ritual. Before the body was wrapped, some of the person's organs were removed, wrapped in linen, and placed in decorated pots called canopic jars. The lungs, stomach, liver, and intestines were each placed in a jar that represented the god that would protect it. The heart was left in the body. Ancient Egyptians didn't realize how important the brain is, so it was removed through the nose and thrown away. Then the body was wrapped in linen and placed in, for upper-class Egyptians, as many as three different coffins, nested one inside the other. These could be cedar or other wood; the outermost one, the sarcophagus, was often made of stone. These and the canopic jars were placed in a stone tomb in the desert for their eternal rest.

Limestone Canopic Jars

Qebehsenuef
(falcon)
intestines

Hapy
(baboon)
lungs

Imsety
(human)
liver

Duamutef
(jackal)
stomach

PRESENT—ORGAN TRANSPLANTS

The ancient Egyptians thought that a dead person's organs could be used in the afterlife. Today when someone dies, we know that their organs can live on, too, but in a different way. Doctors have learned how to transplant them into people whose organs are damaged. Not every organ can be transplanted, but many of the ones we've learned about can be, such as the heart, lungs, liver, pancreas, and kidneys. A portion of the liver, one of the kidneys, and one lobe of the lungs can even be transplanted from a living donor. For all kinds of transplants, the donor and recipient must be a "match," meaning that their size, age, and blood types must be compatible.

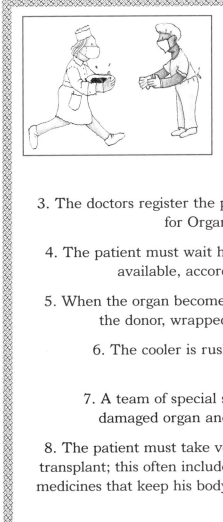

ORGAN TRANSPLANT FROM START TO FINISH

1. A person has a damaged or diseased organ.

2. His doctors decide that the best treatment is a transplant.

3. The doctors register the patient on the United Network for Organ Sharing (UNOS) waiting list.

4. The patient must wait his turn for an organ to become available, according to need and compatibility.

5. When the organ becomes available, it is removed from the donor, wrapped in ice, and placed in a cooler.

6. The cooler is rushed, often by helicopter, to the patient's hospital.

7. A team of special surgeons removes the patient's damaged organ and replaces it with the new one.

8. The patient must take very good care of himself after a transplant; this often includes taking immunosuppressants, medicines that keep his body from rejecting the new organ.

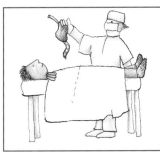

HOW AN ORGAN IS DONATED

1. A person registers as an organ donor.
2. If that person suffers a fatal accident, emergency workers will see that she is a registered donor and contact her family.
3. The donor's family gives consent for her organs to be donated.
4. UNOS is notified of the available organs, and consults its waiting list for a match.

Some organs can be donated by living donors. In the case of living donor donations, the patient and donor are often related or know each other.

Organs: Past, Present, and Future

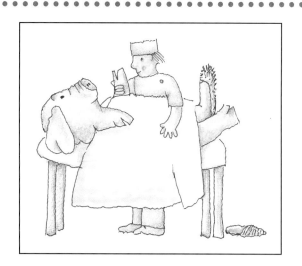

Xenotransplantation is the transplantating of animal organs into human bodies. Pig and human organs are similar in metabolism and size. Because there are so many more patients who need organs than there are donors, scientists are investigating whether using pig organs is a viable option. They are doing research and experiments to find out how to ensure that the human body doesn't reject these nonhuman body parts. With luck, in the future there might be no shortage of organs for those who need them.

Pig Dissection Guide

In here for lungs, liver, spleen, stomach, pancreas, bladder, glands, heart, veins, and arteries.

"If we never took risks with the unknown, we would make little progress in medicine."—David Cooper, M.D., immunologist

Find out more! Find out more! Find out more!

Get your parents' permission to go online— or better yet, take them exploring with you—and check out these great Web sites to keep learning about the amazing world inside each of us.

A Guided Tour of the Visible Human

The Visible Human Project is an amazing way to learn about anatomy. This Web site takes you on a virtual tour of photos of a real human body, letting you explore cross sections of the body's parts and systems. There are also other images to discover, such as X rays and MRIs. **www.madsci.org/~lynn/VH**

HowStuffWorks.com's Life Science Channel

With topics including animals, conservation, evolution, genetic science, and plants, this is a great site to find out about the whole living world and how it relates to you. Ever wonder why humans walk on two legs, what to do if you meet a bear, or whether dogs really are man's best friend? This is the place for the answers—and the place where common myths are debunked. **www.science.howstuffworks.com/life-science**

Human Anatomy Online

Want to learn about even more organ systems? This site gives you a detailed, interactive look at the skeletal, digestive, muscular, lymphatic, endocrine, nervous, cardiovascular, reproductive, and urinary systems. Click on a system part to find out what it is and what it does, or do the opposite: Look up that mysteriously named thing you've always wondered about and see where it actually is in the body and what its function is. **www.innerbody.com**

KidsBiology.com

Part of the Kids Know It network, this Web site will tell you more about biology in general, human biology, and animals. It even has biology games! The human biology section covers major systems of the inner body, including digestive, circulatory, respiratory, excretory, endocrine, and nervous, as well as muscles and bones. **www.kidsbiology.com**

KidsHealth

Find out more about how each of your body parts works through articles, games, Q&A sections, and even minimovies. You can also find recipes, brain-teasing quizzes, and advice, ranging from safety tips to dealing with your emotions. Fun and fascinating! **www.kidshealth.org/kid**

ALVEOLI: Found in the lungs, these are little spaces that serve as the meeting place for the gases we breathe and the bloodstream.

ANATOMY: The study of the structure of living things, as part of the larger science of biology.

ANTIBODIES: Working as part of the immune system, these are proteins that exist in the blood to fend off foreign entities that might be harmful to our health, such as viruses and bacteria.

BACTERIA: Single-celled foreign organisms, which can enter the body and cause illness, be harmless, or do good, depending on the type and on the strength of our immune systems.

BLOOD PRESSURE: A measure of how hard blood is pushing against our blood vessels. It is a very important indicator of health, and blood pressure that is either too high or too low can be problematic.

CHOLESTEROL: A compound occurring naturally in our body's tissues that travels through the blood. Very high cholesterol levels, which can occur from eating fatty foods and not exercising enough, can cause problems for our bodies, especially our hearts.

CINGULATE GYRUS: An area of the brain's folds (each fold is called a gyrus) that helps us feel pain and emotion.

COMMON HEPATIC ARTERY: The artery that delivers oxygen-rich blood to the liver, pancreas, and parts of the stomach and small intestine.

CORPUS CALLOSUM: In mammal brains, the left and right cerebral hemispheres communicate along this region.

DUODENUM: This is the first and shortest part of the small intestine, and much of our digestion takes place there.

ENZYMES: These are important proteins that help chemical reactions occur in the body.

FALCIFORM LIGAMENT: The ligament that divides the liver into its two lobes and anchors it to the diaphragm.

FORNIX: Archlike structures within the brain that help carry signals from the hippocampus.

GLAND: An organ that prepares a substance to be used in the body or to be excreted from the body.

HEPATIC PORTAL VEIN: The vein that carries blood that has traveled from the digestive tract and collected nutrients along the way. The liver will further process and store these nutrients.

HEPATOLOGIST: A doctor who specializes in the liver, pancreas, and gallbladder.

HEREDITY: The process of passing genes and their characteristics from parents to children.

HIPPOCAMPUS: The part of the brain that is important to memory. The hippocampus is often the first part of the brain that Alzheimer's disease affects.

HORMONE: A chemical that acts as a messenger between different cell systems in the body, traveling through the blood. Hormones jumpstart important processes and act as cheerleaders of a sort.

ILEUM: The last part of the small intestine, the ileum absorbs any important materials that the jejunum did not.

INFECTION: Occurs when foreign organisms such as bacteria or viruses enter the body and make the person sick.

INSULIN: A hormone naturally secreted by the pancreas that, when present at healthy levels, helps signal to the rest of the body that a person has all the nutrients he or she needs to function properly.

JEJUNUM: The middle part of the small intestine, the jejunum continues digestion.

LARYNX: The part of the throat where sound is generated; this is sometimes called the voice box. The vocal cords or folds are found here, and the larynx also protects the trachea from food going down the "wrong pipe." Laryngitis—which can be caused by an infection, a cough, or excessive yelling or singing—is an inflammation of the larynx, and it may result in a person's temporarily not being able to speak while the larynx recovers.

MYOCARDIUM: The heart's layer of muscular tissue.

NASAL CONCHA: A long, narrow, and curled bone shelf in the nasal cavity. It is responsible for regulating air inhaled through the nose.

NEPHROLOGIST: A doctor who specializes in the functions and diseases of the kidneys.

OBESITY: A condition in which the amount of fatty tissue built up in the body is so excessive that the person has increased health risks.

OTOLARYNGOLOGIST: A doctor who specializes in the functions and diseases of the ear, nose, and throat; commonly referred to as an ENT.

PHARYNX: A passageway at the very back of the mouth and nasal cavity that connects to the larynx and esophagus. It is very important to our ability to speak.

PITUITARY GLAND: A gland the size of a pea that sits at the base of the brain. It helps to control body processes such as growth, blood pressure, and converting food into energy.

PULMONARY ARTERIES: The blood vessels that carry blood from the heart to the lungs so that the blood can absorb oxygen.

PULMONARY VEINS: The blood vessels that carry oxygen-rich blood from the lungs to the heart so that it can be pumped to the rest of the body.

PULMONOLOGIST: A doctor who specializes in the functions and diseases of the lungs and respiratory tract.

RECTUM: The final portion of the large intestine.

RED BLOOD CELLS: The most common type of blood cells. They carry oxygen from the lungs to the rest of the body.

SINUSES: Spaces within the skull, around the nose, that drain into the nasal cavity.

SPINAL CORD: A thin bundle of nerve cells that is enclosed by the column of bones in the back. It begins at the end of the brain stem and is responsible for transmitting signals from the brain to the rest of the body.

SPLENECTOMY: An operation to remove the spleen.

SPLENIC ARTERY: The blood vessel that carries blood to the spleen.

SPLENIC VEIN: The blood vessel that carries blood away from the spleen.

SUPERIOR VENA CAVA: The large vein that conducts blood from the upper part of the body to the heart.

THALAMUS: A section of the brain that relays sensory information and also helps control whether a person is awake or asleep.

TIBIA: The second-largest bone in the body, located below the knee. It is also called the shinbone.

TISSUE: Similar cells that come together to create a structure with a specific function in the body.

TRAUMA: Injury, whether from being hit or bumped very hard, cut, or otherwise wounded.

VALVE: A part of the body that opens and closes to regulate the flow of fluid from one organ to another.

VIRUS: Extremely small particles that infect cells and cause diseases.

VITAL: Meaning that something is necessary to life.

WHITE BLOOD CELLS: The cells in the blood that fight off infections.